SHORT HANDS, LONG POCKETS

SHORT HANDS, LONG POCKETS

The Informed Guide to Debt and Spending

Eddie Hobbs

CURRACH
PRESS

First published in 2005 by
CURRACH PRESS
55A Spruce Avenue, Stillorgan Industrial Park, Blackrock,
Co Dublin, Ireland

www.currach.ie

3 5 4 .

Cover by SlickFish Design
Cover photograph of author by Tony Keane
Cartoons by Emer O Boyle and Robert Pidgeon
Origination by Currach Press
Printed by ColourBooks Ltd, Dublin

The author has asserted his moral rights.

ISBN 1-85607-926-0

Royalties from the sale of *Short Hands, Long Pockets* are going
directly to The Jack and Jill Children's Foundation. This means
that for every book sold, about €1 of your money goes to the
charity. There is no income to the author.

This publication and software would not have been possible
without the financial assistance of the Credit Union
Development Association (CUDA).

CONTENTS

INTRODUCTION

Bet you're jumpy. Did somebody see you pick up *Short Hands, Long Pockets* from the shelf? Did you tell them at the checkout to gift wrap it? Are you hiding the cover from prying eyes? If it's one thing we Irish hate most it's somebody knowing anything about our dosh – especially when we're in hock! Ever asked your best friend what he or she earned? Like hell you did, that would be like asking a farmer how many cows he had!

The most common question I get asked about RTE's *Show Me The Money* is how participants open up their finances to a national audience – the sheer terror of talking openly about money etched on the face of the enquirer. Yep, the world's great communicators, the designers of the pub and the casual conversation with strangers where religion, politics, sport and life in general are dissected, never talk to each other about money – except maybe in a coded way. It's taboo isn't it?

You don't have to appear on telly to solve your finances, but you probably need to be equally prepared for some hefty shocks as you make your way through the book, track your spending, analyse your borrowing and face the type of decisions needed to get yourself back into the black. For the Jurassic you'll find good old fashioned pencil and rubber formats in the appendix that work just fine and for the more nimble there's intuitive software – The Wonga Wizard – attached that's a doddle to use.

MONEY ARRIVES WITHOUT INSTRUCTIONS

Course money is inanimate, logical, and pretty boring actually. What makes the difference is the huge variety of attitudes and behaviour around it, including shifting values in society in general.

Money doesn't arrive with instructions which didn't really matter too much in the past when we didn't have too much of it or access to other folk's loot, aka borrowing. Before the boom, Ireland as the least developed country in the EU, had a duck-tight credit market. You couldn't really spend more than you earned. You couldn't magnify your lifestyle by taking on a glut of soft credit, and you couldn't get jumbo mortgages with half-baked stories about rent-a-room tenants, dodgy income statements from employers and all the other guff used to qualify for the bloated housing market.

Instead to get a line of credit you usually had to prostrate yourself before a financial priest in one of

the temples Irish banks erected throughout towns and villages as centres of passage to the respectable middle classes. Getting a loan was a privilege in those times: a day out dressed in Sunday best, to go cap in hand to see the omnipotent bank manager, to laugh at his jokes, agree with his admonishments, and accept his judgements.

But as Ireland became the rich man of Europe, lenders have been tripping over themselves to shovel expensive soft credit into the market. You don't even need to leave your home to get a loan – it will come in the post with a snazzy letter and a crisp cheque with the most important words in the world on it – your name. But you can also dial a loan or extend existing loans by email, fax or even text.

It's a boom time for lenders too. Low default rates, and restrictive market conditions make the selling of credit a hugely lucrative business. Stagnant economic growth in middle Europe has kept the cost of borrowing huge sums in the wholesale market for lenders very cheap, at a fraction over 2% into 2005. This stuff can then be cut down into smaller bundles and lent out into a booming peripheral economy at massive margins like four times for car loan debt, five times for overdrafts, and up to nine times for plastic debt – and that's on the main street. Stray off the beaten track and you could be paying interest rates at well over 30% to catalogue companies and money lenders.

> You don't even need to leave your home to get a loan – it will come in the post with a snazzy letter and a crisp cheque with the most important words in the world on it – your name.

The rate of growth in private sector credit, which shoves mortgages together with lifestyle loans, is accelerating at over 25% per year, that's ten times price inflation. While most of the borrowing acceleration is property-related, the data gathered by the Central Bank does not report the massive amount of refinancing of short-term debt into long-term mortgages.

Some economists, especially those employed by lenders, reckon it's all just part of catch-up time for Ireland, but these global figures are masking the difficulties of a large part of the population as it slips further and further into debt, trying to survive on modest incomes, saddled with big mortgages and facing rip-off prices in a high-cost economy where there's been a consistent failure to tackle restrictive markets and state-owned businesses.

No, you can't change that, but what you can do is to get a grip of your own spending and borrowing and then get real smart about how you're going to run your finances thereafter. Like smart enough to see beyond lifestyle debt to decent saving and investment for your future – and it couldn't be more important.

The old age pension, even though it's now supported by the accumulating National Pension Reserve Fund, will at best, only replace about a third of the average industrial wage and that's a little under €10,000 a year. If you don't start accumulating your own private stash you might find you've run out of money before running out of life. So when you're getting cold feet about enduring the pain of transforming your finances consider what you'd look like serving hamburgers in McDonald's on your eightieth birthday. Hey, and don't laugh because life expectancies are lengthening all the time and many of us can reasonably expect the cheque from the President!

To generate a long-term net income of say €20,000 beginning in your mid-sixties you'll need to have accumulated a sobering €500,000 in working assets to be on the safe side. That can all add up from occupational pensions, savings and property and is for a different book – but you can't start a damn thing until you first eliminate lifestyle debt.

That's the thing about this type of debt; it hangs around for years gathering weight and robbing you of the vital time you'll only ever have once, to begin investing for your future. But you'll be amazed at the type of wiggle room you can create and how it can be put to work over the long term, transforming your financial future from one of dependence on family, friends and the state to independence and choice.

THE EXCUSES

It's only human to look for a cop out, to blame economic circumstances, fast pace of life, high property prices, stealth taxes, just about anything, rather than take personal action. For sure there are many things outside of your control that make living within your means harder, but it's not impossible and hundreds of thousands of other people with similar incomes and facing similar challenges manage – so how about you? Are any traits in these caricatures a little too familiar?

The *Dreamers* reckon everything will be alright on the night, that there's a solution just around the corner, that there's no need to plan. These count on big promotions, share options and salaries at work, handouts or inheritances from parents whose homes have swelled in value, and even marriage. Mostly dreamers dream away until it's too late. Favourite senior managers leave, new owners arrive with cost drives, sector downturns happen, parents live into their nineties, nursing home costs force home equity release and destroy inheritances, and the rich admirer gets bored or admits to having no money either. Sadly for dreamers the wake-up call is the alarm clock ringing on the day of the retirement party.

Beloved of credit card companies are the *Champagne Spenders*, the type who wouldn't be seen dead in a car more than a year old, who must have a gold coloured credit card, diamond studded watch, in fact just about everything has to be the most expensive of its kind. The Champagne Man splurges on the latest gadgets, alloy wheels, woofers, plasma screens and sound systems. Even underwear and socks are Hugo Boss. Hell if Hugo Boss did breakfast cereal he'd have that too. For the Champagne Woman shopping is the elixir and there's nothing more pleasing than parading up Grafton Street festooned with top brand shopping bags so everyone knows where you've been. Not for you the budget holiday camping in France, the high heels worn at the last wedding, or, heaven forbid sitting down and working on a pesky budget. Doesn't matter if it's borrowed money so long as you can ape your favourite star on *Sex and the City*.

The *Philosophers* like to say things like 'It's only figures', 'It's all so confusing', 'I hate discussing money.' The socialist philosopher sees the whole money business as a capitalist conspiracy against the working class and would happily nationalise the banks in the morning, but can also recite state benefits faster than you could say the Hail Mary.

The *Save-the-Snails* regard money as quite a grubby thing and drift along never quite sure about how much they're earning or spending so long as it feels good and isn't damaging the environment. These are usually kind, gentle and considerate people, but they rarely plan properly, take on debt from the nicest sounding salesperson and are horrified when lenders are nasty to them when they periodically run short.

But the worst are the *Truly Feckless*. These couldn't give a damn about overspending and live purely in the moment. They see borrowing as a bit of a lark really, loan offers are gifts, credit card limits are targets, letters from solicitors are part of the static you have to take, and anyway if you don't cough up, what can they do? The Truly Feckless always have a big money-making wheeze lined up, one that involves taking huge risks, the higher the better. These are life's gamblers and who reckon they can always die in huge debt and stuff the lenders. These types are colourful and great craic but the Truly Feckless cause mayhem for their partners and children when the pressure mounts, their credit rating evaporates and judgement mortgages attach to the family home.

WATCH YOUR SPENDING

This book comes with an appendix that gives you a format to monitor your spending. Use an old fashioned pencil and rubber to fill it in so you can change things as you go along. Feel free to photocopy as many times as you like and adjust it to fit how you like to fill things in. You can also use The Wonga Wizard software to store your data electronically, as well as give you the flexibility that a pencil and rubber can't.

Before soft credit, most folks did a budget. It was no big deal and often it was mental or done on the back of an envelope. It worked because lifestyles were pretty simple, you couldn't borrow money too easily, and you knew precisely to the nearest penny how long your income would last before the next pay cheque. If you didn't have the cash you just didn't go out. If you wanted to go abroad on holidays you saved – and so did everybody else. It was just fine to tell

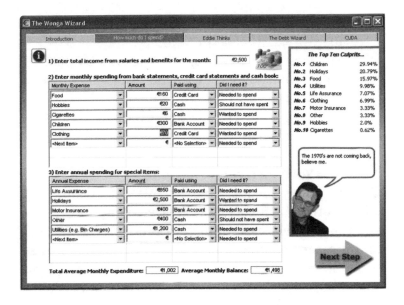

your friends you were skint because they were too.

But when you run a spending analysis these days you need to keep a glass of water and panadol handy. Invariably you'll be horrified by how much you're spending – everyone gets a jolt. You'll equally be amazed just how powerful counting your spending will be.

Here's what to do:

1. Follow the Cash Trail

First you need to run a cash diary for at least a month, and ideally three months. It doesn't have to be anything elaborate. Keep a small notebook in your pocket or handbag and at the end of every day write down what you spent in cash and where. When the first month's done, add your cash spending to your fixed spending on direct debits, cheques, etc in the appendix or The Wonga Wizard. What's likely to strike you is how much cash you spend on:

- Expensive lunches costing €10 per day add up to over €2,300 for the year.
- Smoking 20 a day comes to nigh on €4,000.
- Taxis instead of buses and lifts could easily match your lunch spending.
- Drinking your way through €3,000 to €6,000 in booze and nights out.

2. Add to Your Electronic Spending

Go over your cheque stubs, bank statements and credit card bills for as long as a year if you can and add the monthly costs into your analysis. Here you'll find a record of what you're spending on mortgages, term loans and credit cards. List your debts beginning with the most expensive rate and consider how you could reduce costs by moving down to cheaper deals. In your electronic spending you'll also find foodstuffs, telephone, electricity, waste charges etc. What will hit you is how much you spend on:

- Total debt repayments when it's all added together. If this exceeds a third of your income you'll be under pressure.
- The total you've spent on a couple of holidays a year, weekends and trips away.
- The true cost of modern consumer-driven Christmas and Halloween, as well as what you spend on presents, birthdays and gifts.
- That running a house requires ongoing and unexpected spending on maintenance, repairs and renewals you'd never really thought about.
- That there's not a huge amount left over to invest into savings like the government SSIA scheme, retirement funds and education schemes.

3. Divide your Spending between Must and Mights

This is the hard part and requires honest thinking. Divide your spending between 'must spend' and 'might spend'. Let's get this straight – two holidays a year isn't a 'must spend'. Neither is smoking, meals out, weekends away and luxury shoes and clothes. When you strip it all down your necessary spending should come to a lot less than your net income. The difference is how much you 'might' spend on life's optional luxuries, but with one vital step first.

4. Pay Yourself First

There's likely to be a healthy gap between your net income in the year and your necessary spending total on things like household food, clothing, mortgage, heating, etc. But before you decide where you're going to allocate the surplus across competing optional spends like holidays, entertainment and drinks out, consider paying yourself first by allocating something realistic into your pension fund or other investment. Remember at top rate tax relief every €100 you put into your retirement fund should get you about €170 worth of investment.

5. Now Set Your Budget and Follow It

You've got a finite amount of cash for the year. You know what you must spend on necessities, and you've decided what you'll save. The rest can now be spread across optional areas and once done you're in position to measure your estimates on spending against actual spending by updating your analysis monthly.

No, it was never going to be exciting, but you'll be stunned at just how effective counting your spending can be, how much stress is removed to be replaced by the feeling of being in control once again, and just how painless it is to save money. It's all pretty quick once you get into the habit, it doesn't lead to catastrophic changes in the quality of your life and it won't leave you feeling like a skinflint – just balanced and informed.

But be warned – it's a common mistake to confuse getting a bigger income with the luxury of ditching first principles and abandoning your new habit. Most people who get themselves into the biggest stew aren't the low paid, where budgeting is a must to survive, but those who experience a rise in earnings and chase after ever more expensive lifestyles by creating an ever higher debt mountain.

Every euro you save with good new spending habits is one euro less borrowed at your highest cost of borrowing. When you're overspending your lifestyle debt is rising so the next euro you spend isn't yours, it's borrowed and, in most cases, that means at credit card rates of up to 18%. Here are a few tips, but the list isn't exhaustive so talk to friends and add your own:

- Mistakes are common, so *always check your bills*.
- Write up a *list for your weekly household shop* and stick to it to avoid impulse buying. Never shop without a *preset budget for high price items* like a new coat or shoes.
- *Never shop when you're starving*, eat first otherwise you'll stuff your trolley and your mouth as you shop like there's going to be a meteor strike.
- Ignore the loyalty card which is designed to lure you into the one shop all the time. *Switch to discount stores like Lidl and Aldi for your weekly basics* and top up elsewhere with the remainder. Keep an eagle eye out for bargains like reduced price, promotions, half price and 'buy one get one free' campaigns. New competition arriving is great for price wars so watch out for ways to save money by switching telecom companies, gyms and insurers.
- *Check your weekly household shop for unnecessary spending on silly things* like premium brand dog food, bottled water and fizzy drinks. The dog might like the change to cheaper own brands, a water filter jug is probably just as effective as bottled water and what about giving the kids sugar-free dilutable drinks instead?
- If you're a credit union member ask them for details about *budget payment plans* that smooth out recurring bills like rent, gas, and electricity but *don't cost money to administer*.

WHAT DOES GOOD CREDIT MANAGEMENT LOOK LIKE?

The best way to manage credit is to operate strictly within prudent ratios of debt, and to your capacity to service that debt. For credit cards and other short-term debt ensure that you clear your balance monthly. For overdrafts stay strictly within your overdraft limit. For medium- to long-term loans make sure that repayment is given priority in your income. The following rules of the game are ideally where you want to be.

1. *Periodically find out precisely where you are*. This means summarising all of your assets and liabilities and your income and spending. When this is done express the cost of servicing your liabilities as a percentage of your income. If it is exceeding 33% you are going to run into trouble.
2. Set a strict limit as a percentage of your income for servicing your overall debt. This is your *lifetime limit*. Ideally when you retire the percentage should be zero.
3. People make purchases emotionally whether it's properties, cars, boats or other items like jewellery. Enjoy shopping around but for these things impose a *cooling-off period* on your

purchases. In other words, when you have identified what you want, *never buy it on impulse*. Give yourself at least a week to think it over. Be careful of the 'standing room-only close' the favourite sales technique used to get you to buy immediately, or otherwise you lose the opportunity.

4. *Restrict the number of lines of short-term credit*, ideally to one or two. Multiple use of plastic lines of credit is a guaranteed way to get you into trouble.
5. Examine the different prices for different lines of credit and *always move to the cheapest lines*.
6. *Remove the temptation*. Get a scissors and cut up the lines of credit that you have decided to no longer use. Write to the credit card provider and request it to take you off their mailing list to avoid repeated offers of more credit.

WHEN YOU KNOW YOU'RE IN *REAL* TROUBLE

- An increasing percentage of your income is going to servicing debts.

- You are beginning to *juggle* your lines of credit, delaying payments on some lines, and paying others.

- You are receiving *overdue* notices.

- You only ever make the *minimum* repayment. Outstanding balances never seem to be falling.

- You are beginning to use credit cards *all* the time for things that you used to buy with cash.

- You are beginning to use credit cards for *essentials* like food because you have run out of cash.

- You are going *over* your overdraft limit all the time and incurring surcharges.

- You never really know exactly how much *you owe* and how much you are spending on servicing debt.

- You are *delaying* vital visits to your doctor, dentist, etc., because you are afraid how much it will cost you.

- You *dread* paying for the cost of birthday parties, gifts and especially Christmas.

- You *worry* about the overall level of debt that you hold. All of the time.

- You are beginning to *hide* your bills from yourself, sticking them into a drawer and refusing to open them.

- You are increasingly using *new* lines of credit to pay for old lines of credit.

GETTING OUT OF A DEBT HOLE

There is a huge difference between being poor and being broke. If you are in a debt hole and you are convinced that you are poor you will never get out of it. Once you understand that you are simply broke you are beginning to understand that the position is recoverable. The world is full of examples of people who were once broke and are no longer so. Some of the wealthiest people in the world were once completely broke and insolvent.

1. Set a positive goal for yourself such as going to France with the kids or refitting the kitchen at some point in the future. This is more powerful

than a negative goal such as 'I must get out of debt.' The target may be some way off but give yourself a *reason* to get out of debt. Sometimes visualisation like a photo of what you'd like to achieve is a useful thing to carry around with you, hang on the fridge, or stick to the dashboard.

2. Set a *specific date* to get out of your debt hole but be realistic – it's probably going to take you just as long to get out of debt, as it has taken for you to get into it.

3. Goals are ineffective unless they are written down, so *write up your plan* to get yourself out of the debt hole, and then *share it*. If excessive family expenditure has got you into the hole, then involve members of the family in the plan. Don't carry the entire responsibility on your own shoulders, and certainly don't hide it from the family. Excessive secrecy about debt problems can lead to extreme stress and worry.

4. Summarise your debt position. Put four columns across a piece of paper: *creditor, balance, interest rate and minimum repayment.* Begin completing these columns by starting with the most expensive source of debt. This will be clear from the interest rate. Your objective will be to eliminate the top entry while making minimum repayments to the rest and then work your way down the list taking out the most expensive each in turn. You might refinance your mortgage but accelerate repayments to clear off the added lifestyle debt quickly.

5. Follow the cash trail. Run a cash diary for at least a month, and ideally three months. It doesn't have to be anything elaborate. Keep a small notebook in your pocket or handbag and at the end of every day write down what you spent in cash and where. When the first month's done add your cash spending to your fixed spending on direct debits, cheques, etc. in the *appendix* or *The Wonga Wizard*.

6. Add to *your electronic spending*. Go over your cheque stubs, bank statements and credit card bills for as long as you can go back – up to a year if possible – and add the monthly costs into your analysis. Here you'll find a record of what you're spending on mortgages, term loans and credit cards. You'll also find foodstuffs, telephone, electricity, waste charges, etc.

7. *Divide your spending between 'musts' and 'mights'.* Let's get this straight – two holidays a year isn't a 'must spend'. Neither is smoking, meals out, weekends away, fancy gadgets, and luxury shoes and clothes. When you strip it all down, 'must' spending should come to a lot less than your net income. This is the amount of wiggle room you've got to start attacking your debt mountain.

8. *Sell all liquid assets* immediately such as the cash value of life insurances, cash deposits, bonds, etc., and eliminate as much of the debt as possible. Initially it may not make sense to you to bring your cash deposits to zero, but remember it's nuts to keep money in cash deposit paying you 1% when you've debts costing you as high perhaps as 18%. Is there any other thing you could sell that

you don't absolutely need? What about collections or antiques? Could you get by with just one car? Each car is costing you several thousand euro a year in tax, petrol, insurance, repairs and depreciation.

9. *Look for ways to increase your earnings.* Could you or your partner take on a part-time job? What about asking for a raise if one's due? Is there an opportunity to move jobs and make more money either through increased income or lower travelling costs and reduced childminder fees? Could you rent a room under the tax exempt threshold?

10. *What about selling up and moving home* to another area and freeing up equity to clear your debts and start afresh? If you're a civil servant is there an opportunity to move out of Dublin under the decentralisation scheme with no loss of income?

11. *Reorganise your debt.* Once you've exhausted ways of increasing earnings or reducing debt by selling assets the next step is to attack the debt mountain. There are two ways to do this and which you choose depends on the scale of the task and the wiggle room you've created.

- First try to clear the lifestyle debt on credit cards, term loans and overdrafts by rearranging these into *one lower cost term loan*. Check the interest rates being charged to you on your lines of credit against lower interest rates available from other providers of credit. Often the local credit union is a good place to start but use one that doesn't insist on saving with it while borrowing. If you can *move debt* to other lines of credit at *lower costs* then do so. Look especially at zero interest discounts on credit card balances from competing providers and use the six month window to eliminate the debt. The *Debt Wizard* will help you calculate how quickly you can eliminate the debt mountain at the contribution rate you've identified from your analysis.

- If you can't refinance into a lower cost short-term loan, explore *refinancing your mortgage*. You'll be able to do so if you can convince your lender or a competitor that you've sufficient equity in your home and that the new total mortgage won't exceed 90% of its value. You'll also have to demonstrate that you've sufficient earnings to service the new mortgage. To refinance, first talk to your lender before shopping around. You could, alternatively, use a good mortgage intermediary, preferably one with agencies attached to all thirteen mortgage providers with full disclosure of commissions or, better still, one who works on a flat fee structure, rebating commissions that can be up to 1% of the new mortgage.

Make sure you eliminate the saturated fat you've added to your mortgage. This means upping the normal repayments to eliminate the lifestyle debt you added as fast as you can. This avoids spreading forward your lifestyle debt over many years. For example, let's say your mortgage has eighteen years to run, the balance is €200,000, monthly repayments are €1,250 but you've lifestyle loans of €30,000 elsewhere costing you a bundle.

A revised mortgage of €230,000 would ordinarily cost €1,430 monthly. This looks like magic and is an advertising dream for those pedalling these quick fixes, but what it masks is the total cost of the extra borrowing, a whopping €10,300 in interest over eighteen years. Instead the extra borrowing could be cleared entirely at €545 per month over five years or about €2,700 in interest.

Do your own accelerated mortgage clearance using the *Debt Wizard* or ask your lender to run some examples for you.

12. Keep up rigorous control of your spending until you've eliminated the lifestyle debt and then turn your attention to building up a cash reserve equal to at least six months' lifestyle costs. This becomes your emergency *reserve of cash* which you can use to meet unexpected expenses such as repairs to your home, etc. Commit yourself never again to drift into the awful cycle of overspending and lifestyle borrowing. That doesn't mean you

shouldn't borrow for vital things like house improvements that add value, education that increases your earning power, or on a car because you have to get around; but avoid borrowing for luxuries to finance Christmas, holidays or entertainment.

Why not become an advocate and recommend your friends to follow your lead – because by the time you've taken these twelve steps, believe you me you'll be expert enough to give public lectures!

MOMENTS WHEN INSPIRATION
IS NEEDED

During those dark moments when you're running out of steam, there's probably nothing more motivating than to learn about fellow Irish citizens who've struggled there ahead of you and succeeded. These are real life stories of real people who appeared on *Show Me The Money* and not some writer's concoction. Each has agreed to share their problems publicly and I know, from feedback, that their example has already helped many others. Let me introduce you to:

Liz and Joe,

Paula and David,

Lizzie and Shay.

Liz and Joe

It's 2003 and Liz and Joe, in their early forties, live in a council house that they rent on Dublin's Northside. This is their fourth rented property having started out in 1984 in an inner city council flat as a young married couple. Apart from a honeymoon in Blackpool, Liz and Joe have never been on a holiday together. Liz is a cleaner and Joe is a security guard. Liz earns about €22,000 and Joe €20,500 but expects a pay rise of €5,200 in 2004. Their combined after-tax income is about €35,000. Lisa, their only child, is 16, lives at home and is about to enter the workforce.

Until recent years Liz and Joe didn't have much access to soft credit, and before the boom Joe spent much time unemployed. But times have changed. Problem is that Liz who handles the family finances has come to regard loan offers as a rite of passage to the good times. She's delighted, for example, when one finance house offers to take over some of her loans and give her cash for Christmas – part of the loan of course. But, not too concerned or sensitive to the small print, Liz didn't know that the new loan, at 15% was nearly double the rate of the loans she replaced.

In fact Liz didn't really know too much about their finances but intuitively she felt that things had got out of control. Liz was occasionally depressed and cried about their frenetic money management. When I first met Liz and Joe they didn't know either, how much they owed or how much it was costing them. It came as a shock.

Liz and Joe had managed to accumulate short-term debt of €33,600 or close to a full year's after-tax earnings of €35,000. The interest rates they were paying across three term loans and a credit card ranged from lows of 9% to highs of 16.6% and the servicing costs were now €1,425 monthly or over €17,100 per annum: almost half of their entire year's income.

Liz and Joe resolved to take action. First off they started a cash spend diary and under Joe's eagle eye all spending was monitored against budgets. For Liz that meant giving up her four nights a week social life linked to work, where she was trying to keep up with people in a social set earning a lot more. A five-year term loan of €33,000 – saving over €7,000 per year in cash flow – was negotiated with the Health Services Credit Union. Liz lodged her salary and the credit union managed the regular bill payments through its budget plan. This meant that gas, electricity, council rent and the new term loan were all deducted from Liz's salary, leaving Joe's to fund the rest of their lifestyle. It worked. Joe and Lisa helped Liz to burn her credit card and her €2,500 limit which she had regarded as her cash!

Liz and Joe went from badly-off, uninformed and out of control to broke, informed and back in the game. One year later, still sticking to the cash-only spending, Liz and Joe, who have cut their debt to €27,000, have the option to buy their council house at a 33% discount under the Dublin Corporation Tenant Purchase Scheme fulfilling their life's ambition to own their home and have something to leave for Lisa. The monthly cost of the new mortgage would be less than the combined cost of their council rent and their credit union term loan.

Paula and David

It's 2004 and Paula and David are in a desperate bind. Lenders had lost patience, hard-hitting letters were arriving from solicitors and it looked like their family home would need to be sold to clear all the debts, leaving them and their four young children aged between one and eight in rented accommodation and with a shattered credit rating. Both are aged 29, but only David works outside the home. He brings home about €31,000 as a lorry driver, and they also get child benefit. They owe €77,400 on their mortgage but have added a further €55,000 in term loans, credit cards, hire purchase and even loans from friends and family.

The trouble started when they built their home in 2000 to 2001 and financed the overrun with short-term debt. That, the cost of raising four kids, and poor money management, landed them in a position over which they now had little control. Desperate for help they turned to MABS when things started to boil over in early 2004. Paula and David had consistently broken promises made to their lenders, and it was easy to see why. If they serviced their debts it would absorb the first €24,700 of their earnings! No wonder arrears were building.

MABS negotiated temporary relief from the lenders, paying modest sums and got Paula and David to start budgeting. But even with temporary repayments now down to €12,900 per year, they were struggling badly and the loss of the home looked inevitable. There was only one hope: could their mortgage provider be convinced to refinance the total and save the family home? Paula and David had employed tactics that meant they'd been less than frank with their lenders. It was time to come clean.

Following our first meeting, David and Paula went to their mortgage provider with a plan. If they stuck rigidly to their budget over six months, including MABS-negotiated repayments and cleared mortgage arrears, would the lender be convinced that they'd learned from their mistakes and changed? The lender agreed, after all a distressed mortgage is in nobody's best interest.

The next few months weren't easy. Paula needed to curtail cash spending even more – there was no fat. The family household spending was ruthlessly restricted to €27 per day. The mortgage provider kept a watching brief through periodic reports. It was obvious after four months that they were keeping to their promise. The mortgage provider brought forward the review and agreed to the refinance, a week before Christmas.

The home-related debt of €155,000 was rearranged over thirty years and €15,000 was set up over fifteen years on fixed rates to bring certainty to mortgage costs. House insurance, life assurance and mortgage repayment insurance, which they'd been force to ditch, were added. The yearly cost fell from €24,700 to just under €8,000 or €660 monthly after tax relief of €60. The new repayments were close to their child benefit payments for 2005 leaving most of David's salary intact.

David and Paula left it to the eleventh hour and fifty-ninth minute to save the day. It was a very close-run thing. They came close to losing their family home. The experience has entirely changed their views about borrowing unwisely.

Lizzie and Shay

It's 2005, Lizzie, aged 32, and Shay, 39, live in a rural setting in a home Shay built in his spare time valued at €300,000, with their six children aged between three and ten. Shay earns €52,000 before tax as a machine operator, and that together with child benefit nets to about €50,000 yearly. They've a mortgage of €70,400 and short-term debts, term loans, credit cards and hire purchase of a further €28,600 at interest rates ranging 10% to 18%. Total debt servicing costs absorb about 34% of their net income at €17,300 yearly.

The last loan was €4,000 to get them through Christmas and it's easy to see why. When completing their first budget exercise for me, their total spending for the year was running €11,000 more than their net income of €50,000. It was a straightforward over-spend. The analysis of the spending showed where some of the problem lay.

Lizzie was spending nearly one euro in ten, or €4,700 per year, on four trips a week to bingo and, addicted to fizzy drinks, she was guzzling her way through trays of tins at a rate of €2,500 per year, equivalent to eating ninety spoons of sugar a day. But other cutbacks could also be made. The family shopping was done sporadically in convenience stores with little pre-planning or watchfulness for discounts and bargains.

Lizzie and Shay resolved to live within their means to avoid building up further lifestyle debt. A new lender agreed to refinance their expensive short-term debt at rates between 10% and 18% into a new €99,000 mortgage at 3.45% over the remaining eighteen-year term. But Lizzie and Shay resolved to immediately commence accelerated capital repayments to clear off the fat added to their core mortgage borrowing over four years. This meant upping the normal repayment from a little over €600 monthly by €500 monthly. The cash flow cost of servicing debt was to fall from €17,300 per year to €13,200 per year, allowing scope to accelerate faster and clear the fat added earlier, provided spending could be brought under control.

But spending cutbacks and lifestyle changes were having an equally dramatic impact. Lizzie went to a nutritionist and her doctor, and packed in the fizzy drinks. She cut her bingo down to two nights per week but dropped costs handsomely by getting her relatives to foot her bingo while she drove them as the nominated driver. Lizzie is a non-drinker. Spending on household food also fell dramatically as she did one big shop per week. Their cash diary showed a huge fall in spending from over €3,200 monthly to just under €1,800, that's a saving of €17,600 if maintained over a year.

WHAT'S GOOD AND WHAT'S BAD DEBT?

Debt means borrowing money to do things, but there is clear blue sea between borrowing money to *invest in assets* and borrowing money to *pay for lifestyle*.

Wealth has been created over the ages by borrowing money to invest in assets, particularly working assets like property but people have gone bankrupt by borrowing to pay for lifestyle.

MORTGAGES AND PROPERTY

Borrowing money for property magnifies the rate of return, when the *net cost of borrowing* is substantially less than the capital appreciation and rent for investment property. This gives a *geared* or *leveraged* return. The net cost of borrowing is the interest rate charged less tax reliefs related to interest payments.

Remember the lender just makes the profit margin on the mortgage and doesn't benefit from the rise in value or any fall in value. This goes onto your balance sheet instead. For example, say you had €1million, you bought a property for cash which a year later is valued at €1.1m – you've got a return of 10% (less costs). If you'd put €100,000 down and borrowed €900,000 your €100,000 will have grown 100% (less costs and borrowing). But gearing is a double-edged sword – remember if the value falls 10% the cash buyer's return is -10%, but the heavily-geared borrower in this example is -100%.

> The *real* net cost of borrowing is the difference between the inflation rate and the net cost of borrowing to you.

Inflation also has an important effect on mortgage debt. The *real* net cost of borrowing is the difference between the inflation rate and the net cost of borrowing to you. At a time of high inflation and moderately low interest rates the real net cost of borrowing can even be negative. This means that, the longer you delay debt repayment, the more you *hire* inflation as an agent to erode the real value of the debt outstanding. Irish homeowners emerged from the high inflation 1970s with relatively tiny mortgages because of this effect – paying off mortgages early during negative real inflation is nuts.

Since Ireland entered the euro, base rates and inflation have been a lot lower than we were used to as a small economy needing to keep rates relatively high to protect the punt. The euro base rate into 2005 at 2% is likely to be at the lowest in its range but is likely to hover between 2% and 4% long term. In 2005 Irish inflation is expected to be more like the EU average at 2% or so, but this always has the capacity to move sharply upwards in Ireland which is due to receive over €14billion in maturities from the government SSIA saving scheme over 2006-07.

Increased competition for residential mortgages has driven variable interest rates to as low as 0.8% per annum above the euro base rate of 2%, to as high as 1.5% above it. This has the effect of pricing deals to strong borrowers as low as 2.8% to as high as 3.5% for weaker deals, where loan to value is highest. Even allowing for the small amount of interest relief available this means that most borrowers are experiencing pretty low positive real interest payments, so not too many mortgages are being cleared with lumps of capital. It's pretty effective, however, to apply any surplus from your income to accelerate capital repayments into your mortgage since you will be saving at the net cost of borrowing – a lot higher than you'll get from leaving income surpluses in bank accounts.

You can measure the effect of doing this using the Debt Wizard. If you're not into computers ask your lender to run the numbers for you, identifying how much time could be lobbed off your mortgage if you pushed some more money into it each month.

If the euro base rate rises in steps from 2% to 4% in line with economic recovery in Europe, most Irish home loans will run 5% to 6%, encouraging more people to clear mortgage debt faster.

Refinancing Your Mortgage

When aggressive low cost competitors arrive or interest rates fall to less than your mortgage rate it's understandable that you will consider refinancing. But tread carefully when this proposition is brought to you by somebody else. Frequently the comparisons being made against your position may not take into account the full facts.

And it's important to compare apples with apples. Ensure that any refinancing proposition doesn't play tricks like lengthening the mortgage term to make the proposition look cheaper. At the outset of 2005 the financial regulator IFSRA has not yet introduced a code of conduct to prevent the worst type of advertising in the mortgage refinance market. These promotions, including TV advertising, encourage refinancing and rolling in all short-term debt with promises of huge savings on monthly cash flows and cash back lures.

You should never roll short-term debt into your mortgage unless you've exhausted all the alternatives, including changing your bad spending habits and switching your short-term debt to better deals. Much can be done to lessen pressure on your available net income by, for example, clearing out very pricey loan rates well into double digits with cheaper loans on single digit rates. Remember lifestyle debt should always be cleared as quickly as possible over the short term, so rolling it all into your mortgage is financially incorrect if this means spreading it out over twenty years or more. So don't involve your mortgage in any solution to short-term debt except as a last resort.

> Don't involve your mortgage in any solution to short-term debt except as a last resort.

When mortgage refinancing is promoted, what's not highlighted is the total cost of credit, the huge extra costs you pay by stretching repayments out for many years. As a last resort there's nothing wrong with refinancing to get a better mortgage deal or to sweep in high cost loans – but provided you accelerate capital repayments to clear the added lifestyle debt fat you've put onto your mortgage and you commit yourself to change the overspending behaviour that led to the lifestyle debt first day.

When you're already in a mortgage which has attaching fixed rates you will normally incur a break penalty. Break penalties usually lessen in size the closer you are to the end of the fixed rate period. There are a number of other switching costs which you may have to incur and these are outlined below. Some of these are avoidable if you are refinancing with your existing lender.

MY SWITCHING COSTS		
	My Cost	Example
Redemption Penalties	€	€2,000
Taxes & Stamp Duties	€	€250
Valuation/Appraisal Fees	€	€300
Solicitors Fees	€	€500
Insurance Fees	€	€150
Professional Advisors Fees	€	€300
Any Other Fees	€	N/A
Total Switching Costs	€	**€3,500**

Once you have totalled up switching costs you are now in a position to examine (a) how quickly you will overcome switching costs and break-even, and (b) how much you will save, after the break-even point for the remainder of the mortgage term.

REFINANCING & BREAK-EVEN POINTS

			Example
A.	What am I currently paying each month? (Including all attaching insurances)	€	€850
B.	What would I pay by moving over? (Including all new insurances)	€	€600
C.	My future monthly saving is	€	€250
D.	Total switching costs	€	€3,500
E.	When will I break even? [D ÷ C]	€	14 mths
F.	How much will I save over term? [C x total months remaining after break-even]	€	€3,500

Mortgage Products

Your mortgage is an *asset* in the balance sheet of a lender. You are an investment to the lender. The lender expects to make a profit from this investment. Lenders will expect to earn higher profits where they believe they are taking more risk and that's why there is a range of different interest rates in the mortgage market. Typically the differentiator is the loan-to-value, sometimes also referred to as the debt/equity ratio. This is, very simply, the mortgage as a percentage of the value of the property or security offered to the lender.

In theory a lender's margin is the difference between the rate charged to you, and the cost of funds to them. In the wholesale market the cost of funds is usually a small fraction above the euro base rate, and the difference between it and the variable rate advertised can be regarded as the gross profit margin of the lender.

The Consumer Credit Act 1995 protects borrowers by compelling home mortgages to be presented in a standard format where costs and APR is clearly displayed. This protection does not extend to investment mortgages. Be careful of tricks some lenders play to disguise their true margin like using internal company terms like 'prime rate' upon which an apparent margin is added. These starting points can conceal hidden margins to the lender. Insist on loan offers that refer directly to the euro base rate.

Generally speaking the margins earned on residential mortgages in the US are about 0.8% and about 1% in Britain. Margins are squeezing in Ireland, but are still higher for the average mortgage at 1.25% to 1.5%. The lower cost players in the Irish market include Bank of Scotland who entered the market on 28 August 1999 with a promise to track the euro base rate at a margin no higher than 1.5% per annum, but started off prices at 1% above. The cosy local market was caught cold with margins averaging 2.45% having widened to this corpulent level as interest rates changed when Ireland entered the euro. AIB and EBS have responded strategically by going toe to toe at the cheaper end of the market, but many other lenders still look to recover an extra 0.3% to 0.5% per annum above these bargain basement players.

Variable rate mortgages that contain price guarantees to track the euro base rate by a preset margin are more valuable to you than cheap-looking headline variable rates that afford the lender the discretion to adjust the rate upwards in later years. These offers are often front-ended with distractions like special one-year or two-year discounts. Remember mortgage discounts are lures used to attract borrowers into mortgages whose underlying long-term rates may be higher than tracker mortgages.

If the cost of meeting your mortgage repayments isn't borderline each month, it probably means that it accounts for less than a quarter of your income. This makes variable rates best for you since you'll have the surplus income to ride out the ups and downs of the interest rate market. You can also accelerate capital repayments and shorten the life of the mortgage without penalties applying. Fixed rate mortgages make more sense when any tiny movement upwards in rates could stuff you. Usually this means your mortgage accounts for a third or more of your income, so buying certainty makes sense.

But fixing does mean you're taking a position in the interest rate cycle which may or may not work out cheaper than variable rates, especially if you fix over the long term at high rates. There may also not be scope to accelerate capital repayments into your fixed rate mortgage without incurring the early exit penalties lenders characteristically attach to these deals. You could decide to split your mortgage into two accounts, one fixed and one variable, attacking the variable account with accelerated repayments.

Don't compare *fixed* mortgage rates against short-term money markets. You are not comparing apples with apples. In order to get an idea of the lender's margin for a fixed rate mortgage you need to compare it against what the lender could get, if it were to place the money instead in eurobonds over the same term as the fixed rate.

For example, if the fixed rate on offer is a ten-year rate ask your lender for the current yields to redemption for ten-year eurobonds. After he's picked himself up off the floor you both might be surprised to find that the lender's margin is higher on the fixed deal than for its variable deal due to lower competition.

Normally fixed rates are higher than variable rates, reflecting the usual upward sloping yield curve, but this is not always so. When fixed rates on offer are less than variable rates on offer, the yield curve is sloping downwards, i.e. there is an expectation of falling interest rates.

Most repayment mortgages reduce the outstanding balance monthly, but new versions are emerging that do so daily and encourage you to run your salary through an attaching current account. This allows the credit balance in the current account, and which will decline over the month as you spend the money, to be offset against your mortgage. Essentially it means that your cash is investing at the mortgage rate which will be a lot higher than zero rates for most current accounts or tiny rates for small deposits. Neither is DIRT payable. More players are likely to offer these current account mortgages, cutting margins and lowering rates as they gain in popularity. They're only effective, however, if you can begin to accumulate surplus income in the current account that builds over time and knocks years off a mortgage.

The Debt Wizard will help you model your mortgage. You can quickly see how much your mortgage will cost at different interest rates and over different time periods. By putting in an existing mortgage balance, term remaining and monthly cost, the Debt Wizard will show you how many years you can knock off your mortgage by upping your monthly repayments – even a slight acceleration can cannibalise the outstanding debt at an amazing speed. Check it out. If you're computer illiterate ring your lender and ask them to run the scenario for you.

Interest-only mortgages were once the preserve of the ultra-high net worth. No recurring capital repayments are required. These have become increasingly available in the mass market, but should only be used by borrowers with strong balance sheets and should never be used as an alternative to a repayment mortgage on a home simply because the repayment mortgage is dearer. This type of muddled thinking drove the misselling of endowment mortgages in the past. In the wrong hands these can encourage risky property speculation by borrowers who simply don't have the financial strength to deal with the aftermath of an investment that goes sour.

The capital borrowed with interest-only mortgages ultimately has to be repaid. These mortgages are used as sources of finance by syndicated groups that purchase large properties, borrow usually 60% to 70% of the value and match the rent to the borrowing, but without pledging the personal assets of the investors, an  arrangement called non-recourse debt. Interest-only mortgages are also used by professionals such as solicitors, doctors and dentists to acquire a practice premises with promises to repay the debt in the future from the accumulating values of pension investments. Full time professional investors with large property portfolios rarely use repayment mortgages, favouring interest-only mortgages and clearing debt by selling off properties.

THE ANATOMY OF CREDIT

Credit falls into two categories, open-ended credit such as credit cards, charge cards, etc., and closed-ended credit such as mortgages, car loans, etc.

Often called *revolving credit*, open-ended credit provides a line of credit which you can tap into and pay back on an ad hoc basis. Don't be misled by the headline interest rate advertised. The important figure is the *APR (annualised percentage rate)*. In Ireland, just like in the US and Europe, the advertising of APR is a legal requirement. APR helps borrowers compare bananas with bananas. Lenders can use different methods to calculate interest but APR levels the pitch between different offerings.

In open-ended credit the *average daily balance* is commonly used. This is created by adding all of the daily balances over a month and then dividing by the number of days in the month. This may, or may not, include new purchases made during the month. Some lenders prefer to use a combination of the current and past billing cycle in order to calculate the balance.

Don't ignore *annual fees*. These are flat fees payable for the privilege of using the line of credit. Lenders can charge very high fees on designer credit products, justifying these by the additional services they provide or for freebies such as discounts on hotel accommodation, free air miles, the replacement of lost or stolen goods, etc. Some products provide emergency help services for medical problems. Credit providers differentiate between one product and another using card colours such as gold and platinum.

The *minimum payment* varies from one line of credit to another, and can also vary on the basis of the lender's view of your credit worthiness. *Hidden* transaction fees may be charged much like bank charges on current or checking accounts, by debiting money against your balance based on the frequency of usage. Late payment fees can be charged when you are a few days late with your minimum payment. *Grace periods* refer to the number of days given to you in which to make the minimum payment notified in your statement.

CLOSED-ENDED CREDIT

Closed-ended credit provides a fixed amount of money usually for a specific purchase. The loan repayment is set over a specific period of time, and hence the term closed-ended. Typical purchases include cars, kitchens, furniture, etc., and the lenders are banks, building societies, credit unions and finance houses.

Closed-ended loans are based on either fixed rates of interest or on variable rates (also called adjustable rates). Fixed rates guarantee that you will pay the same rate of interest for the term of the loan whereas variable rates will move up and down in line with changes in the euro base rate. The short-term loan market in Ireland has not evolved competitively enough to see the introduction of tracker term loans or deals that offer caps or ceilings that limit the level to which the interest rate can rise, but this will happen eventually.

SECURITY

There is a big difference in price between secured and unsecured credit. Secured loans means that the lender has an assignment over some of your assets such as your home, stocks, bonds, etc. When security is provided to the lender this should be reflected in a lower interest rate than where no security is assigned, i.e. an unsecured loan.

Short-term lines of credit such as credit cards and overdrafts up to certain limits have higher rates of interest because the debt is usually unsecured. Just because a debt is unsecured doesn't mean that the lender will not seek to recover the monies owed should you default on the loan. Unsecured loans do not mean that your assets are not exposed, it simply means that the lender does not have a direct assignment over your assets.

> You should always separate your source of short-term finance from your source of long-term debt.

As a general rule you should always separate your source of short-term finance, whether it is working capital for a business in the form of an overdraft or credit cards to fund lifestyle, from your source of long-term debt such as mortgages.

Lenders regard loans as investments upon which they expect to make profits and can be very quick to protect their position if they feel that your ability to service your debts is in doubt. When borrowers arrange their overdrafts, credit cards, residential mortgage and investment mortgages with one bank, the bank may attempt to cross-secure all of the debt against the assets held in the fine print of loan agreements.

Remember the window to financial distress is your current account. Here a bank will quickly see a crisis unfolding. If a bank feels it's threatened it will close down your lines of credit. It makes sense to arrange long-term mortgages with lenders other than those you use for short-term debt. Once a mortgage provider receives periodic payment on a long-term loan it will be content and will have no access to information on the state of your current finances.

DON'T EVER IGNORE YOUR LENDER

A common mistake made when borrowers run into cash flow difficulties and default on repayments is to ignore their lender's communications. This is probably the worst thing you can do. Your silence guarantees that the crisis loan is now escalated within the strict procedures established by lenders to deal with defaulters. Inevitably a failure by the lender to reach you or come to some agreement about repayments will result in the file being handed to their solicitors or a debt collection agency. These can make life miserable with constant harsh reminders to pay up or face a court judgement which could result in a visit by a sheriff appointed by the court to confiscate goods to the value of the outstanding debt.

In addition surcharge interest can be added to the outstanding balance swelling its weight.

Lenders expect a certain percentage of borrowers to run into difficulties and have procedures established to work with their customer through the difficulty. This makes good business sense for the lender because it's a lot cheaper than mounting legal action to recover bad debts. Most lenders will agree to lower repayments temporarily but won't agree to anything if you just block them off.

WHEN HELP IS NEEDED

If your debt has deteriorated beyond the point where you can apply the DIY tactics contained in this book, you need professional help to renegotiate your debts and seek write-offs where possible. If your lifestyle debts are more than once your entire income for the year and you've no equity in property, you need to see an expert fast.

Fortunately there is help available. Established to deal with debt and budgeting during harsher times the government-sponsored Money Advice & Budgeting Service (MABS) provides a free and expert service for crisis debt and is respected by the lending community as a good budgeting counsellor and reliable arbitrator. MABS also has strong links to the credit union market. It favours solutions that do not involve remortgaging which isn't always workable. Accountants are also used to professionally represent clients in debt rescheduling and negotiation and will charge for their service.

HOW LENDERS APPROACH
LENDING MONEY

Loans are *assets* in the balance sheet of a *lender*. To determine whether or not they should invest in you, and what margin of profit they require in order to make the investment give a return appropriate to the level of risk, lenders examine the Three Cs – Collateral, Capacity, and Character.

Collateral

Lenders will ask you for a formal or informal statement of affairs, akin to a balance sheet. This summarises the total level of assets and liabilities that you hold. For secured loans they will seek collateral at least one ninth higher than the residential mortgage requested, i.e. a loan to value of 90% and up to twice as high where the loan is used to invest in speculative investment like shares.

They will pay close attention to the ratio between your liquid assets such as fixed interest securities, cash value of life insurances, shares, etc., and to your short-term liabilities such as credit card debt, car loans, etc. They will use a number of different financial ratios, including the *current ratio*.

The current ratio is your current assets divided by your current liabilities. Ideally this should be zero or at worst 4:1. Where lenders see that your current liabilities and your current assets are of equal size, i.e. 1:1, they will regard you as a poor risk.

Capacity

Although most borrowers believe that lenders concentrate on collateral, this is not their top priority. Their first priority is your *capacity to meet repayments on the debt.* This is because the last thing lenders want to do is to spend large sums of money on legal fees to recover their debt by seizing part or all of your assets. It is for this reason that they are very curious about your earned income and unearned income from investments. They will be also keen to learn how much you are already spending elsewhere on servicing debt and how much your lifestyle is costing.

Sharply rising property values, lower interest rates and increased competition for mortgage assets has liberalised borrowing, but the change is fraught with risk as borrowers mistake jumbo mortgage offers with their capacity to repay. As a rule your residential mortgage repayments shouldn't account for more than 28% of your annual income, and servicing all debt including lifestyle loans shouldn't exceed a third of it, allowing two-thirds to pay for your lifestyle and savings.

> Your residential mortgage repayments shouldn't account for more than 28% of your annual income, and servicing all debt including lifestyle loans shouldn't exceed a third of it.

While we continue to experience historically low interest rates these important ratios may look overly cautious, but when rates rise by a percent or two, those currently in the red zone, applying over 40% of income to servicing debt will slip up to the black zone of 50% plus. As a general rule if your debt is absorbing over a third of your income you are likely to take on more and more debt in the absence of the type of rigorous lifestyle budgeting. A percent or two increase in interest rates might sound innocuous but remember a 1% increase on a rate of 4% is an increase of 25%.

Character

Character is the next most important measure signified by your credit rating. Lenders rely on the Irish Credit Bureau and their past experience with you to provide a rating. Credit bureaus measure whether or not you have exhibited good character in meeting repayments on previous loans and will score you accordingly. You are entitled to a copy of any  record held by the Irish Credit Bureau and it's worth checking in advance of any new credit application especially for errors.

OVERCHARGING

It would be unwise to assume that product providers do not make mistakes. Professional services undertake independent audits of credit products such as overdrafts and mortgages especially after a period of irregular repayments when surcharge interest may have been applied. Overcharging is frequently reported from these exercises. They rarely reveal undercharging. So what can go wrong?

Overdraft contracts allow a lender to impose a *surcharge* on top of the normal rate of interest charged when users go over the overdraft limit. But this surcharge may remain live for prolonged periods after the balance has fallen back under the overdraft limit. When interest rates change, typically downwards, the surcharge may continue to apply

Transaction charges and other fees can be applied which do not form part of the credit agreement. These and other matters can be difficult to spot. This is particularly so because the interest charged on overdrafts is based on the cleared balance, and not on the uncleared balance that appears on the checking or current account statement. Specialist software and service providers can audit the interest charged by allowing for the amount of time transactions take in the clearing system.

Credit cards can record incorrect amounts for purchases made and deductions on your card by merchandise providers to whom you have returned defected goods. You should always check your statements including for identity theft and unauthorised use.

SOURCES OF LIFESTYLE DEBT

Credit cards are issued by a range of providers such as banks, retailers, brokerage firms and other financial firms. They provide you with a preset credit limit.

Credit card providers base the interest charge on a variable rate. This rate normally only moves when there is a general movement in interest rates. Unhappily the experience has been that rate cuts have not been fully passed through to borrowers and Irish credit card rates are very high, typically in the range 14% to 18%. Remember the cost of money to the lender in the wholesale market is a little over 2% and the margin they enjoy is applied monthly to about €1 billion in uncleared credit card balances.

You can use the card to purchase goods and services or to obtain a cash advance up to the credit limit. Credit cards require a minimum periodic payment which is calculated on the basis of your overall credit limit and the amount of your balance. Interest is charged on your balance using various methods described earlier. The most common is the average daily balance.

The best known global provider is Visa which is a franchise operation that licenses different financial firms worldwide to offer cards under the Visa brand. This allows a franchisee to set its own prices and lending guidelines within the parameters prescribed by Visa. The market has expanded greatly with credit cards now provided by retail stores, motor manufacturers, and utilities.

The mismanaged credit card is the gateway to serious debt problems simply because it's so easy to use and has low minimum repayment thresholds. Remember, all you have to do is to raise your arm from your wallet or handbag, and swish, you've just added another loan to your burgeoning portfolio. One in every two Irish credit card users mismanage their card by not fully clearing the balance each month. It's an invidious system because even if you leave a euro behind on your card, come interest settlement day you'll be charged interest on the full debt. Let's say your balance is €2,052 and you write a cheque for a round figure like €2,050 – you'll be charged interest on €2,052 even though there's only €2 left on the card.

Because about one in every two Irish credit card users don't clear their debt each month their credit card is the gateway to increasing their debt girth. That's why on *Show Me The Money* I encourage their destruction in tandem with an overhaul in spending and their replacement with lower rate debt and cash-only spending. I also encourage leveraging the competitive forces of the market by surfing it every six months to competitors offering 0% rates for balances transferred and new purchases.

This can save a bundle. Consider that €5,000 outstanding on a credit card at 18% costs €900 for the year just to stand still, whereas surfing at the cost of two phone calls six months apart saves €900.

A *debit card* like Laser is an electronic purse linked directly to your current account. There is no credit limit. The limit is set by how much cash you have in your account and any attaching overdraft limit you've agreed with your bank. Where you use a debit card while in overdraft you're still borrowing at rates likely to be between 4% and 8% cheaper than most credit cards. Debit cards transfer money from your account directly to the bank account of the firm from whom you are purchasing goods and services. In time debit cards will not be exclusively linked to current accounts but will be pre-purchased by users for set sums of money to pay for things like telephone calls, or to facilitate international travellers to meet the cost of travel electronically.

Overdrafts were the traditional gateway to trouble for over-spenders until credit cards with even more expensive rates arrived to replace them. An overdraft is formally applied for to your bank and attached to your current account. It is typically reviewed yearly but can be withdrawn at any time especially if the bank feels your over-extended elsewhere. The overdrawn overdraft is probably the most troublesome interface between banks and customers. When you go over the overdraft limit you break the contract with your bank.

This doesn't automatically mean that cheques you wrote will be dishonoured by the bank but you will face surcharge interest of an additional 6% at least, plus referral fees many times the norm. Overdraft rates range from 9% to 11% so overdrawn borrowers will find themselves facing into rates between 15% and 17% plus referral fees. If you use overdrafts always talk to your bank. Keep your bank informed especially if you're going to go overdrawn and let them know how and when you'll clear the debt. If it becomes a hardened debt that you can't pull down swiftly your bank might suggest switching it to a lower cost short-term loan, but whatever you do don't ignore your bank – keep talking to them.

Charge cards, also called travel and entertainment cards, differ from credit cards by requiring the user to clear the total balance at the end of each month. The best known is American Express. Just like credit cards you are borrowing money in the short term to purchase goods and services to pay for them later. Typically charge cards have a range of annual fees linked to a range of benefits and services provided. Unlike credit cards they do not provide a direct spending limit. The limit is calculated by tracking your spending. Where users do not clear the full balance outstanding at the end of each month, a line of credit is provided at high rates of interest similar to credit cards.

Term loans, also called instalment loans, are the most common type of short-term loan. These are used to buy things like cars, computers, furniture, etc., and are usually unsecured. Payments are made monthly over terms such as three to five years and interest rates settle somewhere between homeloan mortgage rates and overdraft rates. At the front end most of your monthly repayment is interest, and at the back end most of it is capital. Usually term loans can be cleared early by simply clearing the current balance but some instalment loans may charge penalties for early repayment. Increased competition is helping to drive down margins in the term loan market but still rates are high with cheapest deals ranging between 7% and 9% into 2005.

Be careful of discretionary pricing. Some players headline their cheapest rate in their advertising but adjust the rate up sharply, depending on your relative financial strength when you apply. Invariably, unless you're pretty well heeled you'll get a disappointingly higher rate and which could range up to 17%.

Credit union term loans can sometimes come with a stipulation that you need to save for a few months with the credit union before qualifying for a loan – but this can be waived. Other credit unions look for savings while repaying debt and, unless you want to save as well it's best to avoid these arrangements and push for a term loan only. The credit union movement plays a vital part in Ireland's financial marketplace and their mutuality and community-based ethos makes them very different to commercial lenders, e.g. when loans become distressed. Because of the strain of taking in so much on deposits when interest rates fell after Ireland entered the euro, credit unions need to lend a lot more, and are well worth talking to, but always check the rate.

These can vary from as low as 5% with some credit unions to highs of 12% but usually there is scope for interest refunds following AGMs. Unhappily the Credit Union Act 1997 has allowed restrictive and anti-competitive market sharing practices to continue that prevents you from dealing with a credit union outside of your area. If opening times are poor and rates uncompetitive, check out if you can enter affinity group credit unions through a family member. What the credit union can offer is pretty unique – a combination of reasonable rates, local decision making and flexibility when things go wrong or off track. The credit union, as a community-based mutual, is founded along democratic principles and getting involved as an active member isn't a bad way of getting to know your area and making new friends.

Margin loans are available through stockbrokers allowing investors a line of credit through which to buy securities such as equities, bonds, etc. Typically margin loans are on a variable rate basis, moderately above the cost of funds to the broker. They are usually linked to short-term government bonds or base rates. Stockbrokers provide this facility in order to encourage clients to invest more money in securities, setting the credit limit up to 50% of the value of securities already held.

Service loans are typically used by insurance

companies in Ireland but can also be used by utilities such as electricity providers and telephone companies. You will be provided with a way to smoothen out your payments monthly or with a period of time in which to pay the bill. Many people use smooth payment offers from insurers to spread motor and house insurance costs over 10 months without ever checking the small print. These can be loan agreements with borrowing rates of up to 15% and you'd be much better off paying up-front for the year or, at least, paying for it out of a cheaper overdraft or one-year term loan.

People put so much effort into changing cars and getting good deals they frequently make a hash of the finance arranged. It's not uncommon, especially when finance is arranged through car dealerships for buyers to confuse their lease or contract hire agreement with a term loan. The two are distinctly different. Leases sold with bargain cars at APR over 30% provide handsome profits for the car dealership in commissions paid by leasing companies.

> People put so much effort into changing cars and getting good deals they frequently make a hash of the finance arranged.

THINK LEASING, THINK RENTING

One of the most common mistakes borrowers make is to confuse term loans with leases and similar type finance, often assuming that the finance they've arranged at the forecourt or electrical shop is a term loan rather than a lease or hire purchase agreement. This is a mistake that leads to shock when they try to break out of the finance early or fall behind in payments and find the driveway empty – and the car repossessed!

The best way of understanding leasing is to consider that an asset like a car or fridge freezer consists of three parts: ownership, depreciation (loss in value) and interest costs when financing is used.

When you use term loans you pay for all three parts.

With leasing you are paying only for the use of the car. You pay for its depreciation and interest but not its ownership, unless you buy out the residual value with your very last payment which explains why there always appears to be an extra month, for example 37 months or 61 months. In Ireland, hire purchase tends to be used more by consumers either spreading the buy out over the full term or paying it off in a balloon repayment at the end, while companies choose to lease or contract hire.

> With leasing you are paying only for the use of the car. You pay for its depreciation and interest but not its ownership, unless you buy out the residual value with your very last payment.

Contract hire is typically used within motorcar ranges and allows a frequent change of car. Essentially you rent the car for a period of time from a fleet company who broker the finance, by paying a deposit, making monthly payments and agreeing mileage limits. When the agreement expires you don't own the car, but you may have options to buy it at an agreed value linked to the popularity of the car, the mileage and depreciation.

To Lease or Loan?

This is a tricky one, but generally speaking, you're probably better off using term loans if it's likely that you'd want to break out of a lease, hire purchase or contract hire early. The cost of breaking out can be obscured by the offer of a rollover finance agreement for the next car, but, remember you'll pay one way or the other.

With a variable rate term loan you own the car from day one, and simply pay off your bank or credit union over time. If you clear the loan early there are no penalties and if you fall behind in repayments, while you might get a solicitor's letter from the bank or credit union, neither, (unless they've secured a court order), will arrive at your driveway to repossess their property because they don't own your car – you do.

For people in business there can be significant tax differences between these different types of finance agreements and this should be referred to your tax advisor.

APPENDIX

THE WONGA WIZARD

So, there you are in front of your PC. You will find a slot for disks. Make sure it is empty, much like you would with a video recorder. Now, take the disk with the funny logo side facing up and slide it in. That wasn't too hard was it? Your PC will automatically load. You should hear a whirring sound and, low and behold, The Wonga Wizard comes up on the screen. If it hasn't, try plugging in your computer. Or ring a kid.

If you need help at any stage using the software, click on the 'i' icon in the top left corner of the screen.

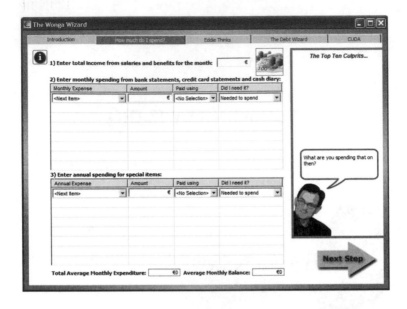

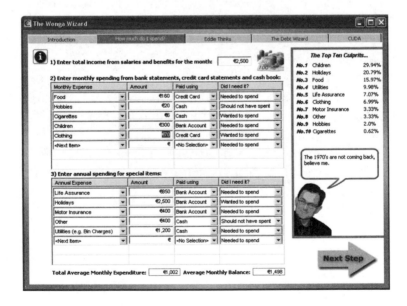

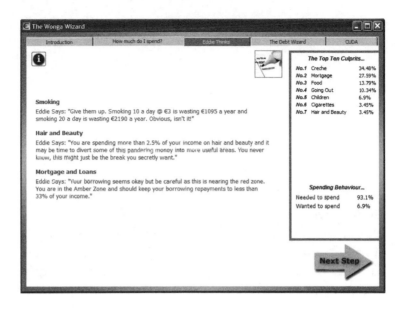

The Wonga Wizard

| Introduction | How much do I spend? | Eddie Thinks | The Debt Wizard | CUDA |

The Top Ten Culprits...

No.1	Creche	34.48%
No.2	Mortgage	27.59%
No.3	Food	13.79%
No.4	Going Out	10.34%
No.5	Children	6.9%
No.6	Cigarettes	3.45%
No.7	Hair and Beauty	3.45%

Smoking

Eddie Says: "Give them up. Smoking 10 a day @ €3 is wasting €1095 a year and smoking 20 a day is wasting €2190 a year. Obvious, isn't it!"

Hair and Beauty

Eddie Says: "You are spending more than 2.5% of your income on hair and beauty and it may be time to divert some of this pandering money into more useful areas. You never know, this might just be the break you secretly want."

Mortgage and Loans

Eddie Says: "Your borrowing seems okay but be careful as this is nearing the red zone. You are in the Amber Zone and should keep your borrowing repayments to less than 33% of your income."

Spending Behaviour...

| Needed to spend | 93.1% |
| Wanted to spend | 6.9% |

Next Step

MY BUDGET

Eddie Says

Put your *monthly* current spend in column 1. *Annualise* it in column 2. Use column 3 for any notes. To start off use your *best guess* when you're not sure. Afterwards you will have to run a *cash diary* for at least a month and ideally three months to get a handle on casual cash expenditures. These are highlighted with (?).

The rest should be obvious from credit card bills, cheque stubs and bank statements – direct debits and standing orders. Start there, i.e. the records you can check easily, ideally look over the last twelve months if you still have the records and then run the cash diary for the rest.

Where you're paying for something yearly, don't ignore it. Enter it as a monthly cost.

	Expenditure Analysis	What's Spent Monthly	What That is Annually	Notes
1.	**Housekeeping Expenses**			
	Gas			
	ESB			
	Oil			
	Solid Fuel			
	Rates			
	Telephone			
	Help-in-House			
	Garden/Gardener			
	Repairs/Renewals			
	Houschold Alcohol (?)			
	House Insurance			
	Other Insurance Premiums			
	Laundry & Dry-Cleaning (?)			
	TV/Video Rental			
	TV Licence			
	Housekeeping, Food, etc. (?)			
	Pet Food (?)			
	Holiday Home Expenses (?)			
	Toiletries (?)			
	Newspapers/Magazines/Books (?)			
	Lotto/Betting (?)			
	Medicines (?)			
	Other (specify) (?)			
	Sub-Total	€	€	

	Expenditure Analysis	What's Spent Monthly	What That is Annually	Notes
2.	**Personal Expenses**			
	Drinks Out (?)			
	Meals Out (?)			
	Snacks (?)			
	Cigarettes & Tobacco (?)			
	Own Clothing & Footware (?)			
	Partner's Clothing & Footware (?)			
	Hair & Beauty (?)			
	Xmas & Birthday Presents (?)			
	Holidays including Weekends			
	Subscriptions			
	Sports/Hobbies/Entertainment (?)			
	Health Insurance			
	Pocket Money/Misc Expend. (?)			
	Gifts to Charities			
	Travel & Other Personal Expenses (?)			
	Study (?)			
	Work-related (?)			
	Sub-Total	€	€	

	Expenditure Analysis	What's Spent Monthly	What That is Annually	Notes
3.	**Children & Grandchildren**			
	Babysitter's Fees (?)			
	Clothing & Footwear			
	Education Expenses			
	Pocket Money			
	Other Children's Expenses			
	Sub-Total	€	€	
4.	**Cost of Servicing Debts**			
	Mortgage on Residence			
	Hire Purchase			
	Bank Loans/Bank Charges			
	Alimony/Maintenance			
	Other Similar Expenses			
	Sub-Total	€	€	
5.	**Motoring Expenses**			
	Car Tax			
	Car Insurance			
	Petrol/Diesel & Oil (?)			
	Services & Repairs			
	AA Subscription			
	Depreciation* & Other Expenses			
	Other			
	Sub-Total	€	€	

* To calculate the cost of depreciation use 20% of original market value of the car(s) as an annual cost. Remember you're going to have to replace it sometime and depreciation is simply a way of spreading out this real cost.

	Expenditure Analysis	What's Spent Monthly	What That is Annually	Notes
6.	**Investments & Life Assurance**			
	Life Assurance Premiums			
	Pension Contributions			
	Govt Savings Scheme (SSIA)			
	Building Society			
	Instalment Savings Plan			
	Business Expansion Scheme			
	Other Savings & Investment			
	Sub-Total	€	€	
7.	**Professional Fees**			
	Accountant			
	Architect			
	GP (?)			
	Dentist (?)			
	Optician			
	Osteopath			
	Physiotherapist			
	Solicitor			
	Veterinary Surgeon			
	Other			
	Sub-Total	€	€	

Income Less Expenditure Summary

	What I Get Per Year – Before Tax	What I Get Per Year – After Tax	Notes
This is My Income – Summary			
Earned Income – PAYE (SCH E)			
Earned Income – Private (SCH D)			
Bonus/Commission/Fees/Overtime			
Rental Income			
Investment Income			
Dividend Income			
Child Benefit			
Other Income Including Cash (DETAIL)			
Total Income	€	€	

	What's Spent Monthly	What That is Annually	Notes
Expenditure – Summary			
Housekeeping Expenses			
Personal Expenses			
Children & Grandchildren			
Cost of Servicing Debts			
Motoring Expenses			
Investment & Life Assurance			
Professional Fees			
Total Expenditure	€	€	
Income Less Expenditure	€	€	

WORKING NOTES

WORKING NOTES

WORKING NOTES

WORKING NOTES

WORKING NOTES

WORKING NOTES

THE JACK AND JILL CHILDREN'S FOUNDATION

The Jack and Jill Children's Foundation is a remarkable charitable organisation that provides respite care to over 200 Irish families who have little babies that are born with severe intellectual and physical damage, and are in huge need of the help of its full-time team of paediatric nurses. Founded by Jonathan Irwin and his wife, Mary Ann O'Brien, following the death of their 22-month old baby, Jack, in 1997, it now spends about €1.6 million annually to help other families who are experiencing the unique difficulties that this special situation brings. For every retail copy sold of *Short Hands, Long Pockets* about €1 of your money goes directly to The Jack and Jill Children's Foundation. There is no income to the author. Many thanks for your support.

Eddie Hobbs

Contact:
The Jack & Jill Children's Foundation
Johnstown Manor, Johnstown
Naas, Co. Kildare
Tel 045 894538 • Fax 045 894558
Web www.jackandjill.ie

CUDA
credit union development association

The Credit Union Development Association (CUDA) is a recently incorporated representative/ development association for credit unions in Ireland. Its current membership includes both community-based and employer-based credit unions who in aggregate terms comprise of €1.75 billion in assets and more than 350,000 members.

CUDA's mission is to act as a catalyst for the growth, development and expansion of credit unions as the ethical alternative to profit-driven financial institutions, by identifying and meeting the representative, service and development needs of progressive credit unions in a value-for-money manner, while operating to the highest standards of integrity, accountability, transparency and trust.

Contact:
CUDA
12 Camden Row, Dublin 8
Tel 01 479 0530 • Fax 01 479 0531
Email bdoylecuda@eircom.net